Wildlife Scientists

Reading and Understanding Graphs

Dawn McMillan

Wildlife Scientists

Reading and Understanding Graphs

Dawn McMillan

Publishing Credits

Editor
Sara Johnson

Editorial Director
Emily R. Smith, M.A.Ed.

Editor-in-Chief
Sharon Coan, M.S.Ed.

Creative Director
Lee Aucoin

Publisher
Rachelle Cracchiolo, M.S.Ed.

Image Credits

The author and publisher would like to gratefully credit or acknowledge the following for permission to reproduce copyright material: cover, The Photo Library/Alamy; title, Shutter Stock; p. 4 (left), Photos.com; p.4 (right), Harcourt Index; p.5, Dr. Ian Stirling; p.5 (inset), Photo Disc; p.6, Corbis; p 8–9, Corbis; p.9 Corbis; p.10–11, Dr. Ian Stirling; p.12–13, Bigstock Photo; p.14–15, Harcourt Index; p.16, Corbis; p16 (inset), Photo Disc; p.17, Corbis; p.18–19, Photos.com; p.19 (inset) Corbis; p20–21, The Photo Library; p.22–23, Getty Images; p.23 (inset), Corbis; p.24 (inset) Newscom; p.24–25, Getty Images; p.25 (inset), Harcourt Index; p.26–27, Photo Disc; Big Stock Photo; p.29

While every care has been taken to trace and acknowledge copyright, the publishers tender their apologies for any accidental infringement where copyright has proved untraceable. They would be pleased to come to a suitable arrangement with the rightful owner in each case.

Teacher Created Materials

5301 Oceanus Drive
Huntington Beach, CA 92649-1030
http://www.tcmpub.com
ISBN 978-0-7439-0889-4
© 2008 Teacher Created Materials, Inc.
Reprinted 2012

Table of Contents

Wildlife Scientists

Do you love animals and being outdoors? You might like to be a **wildlife scientist** (SY-uhn-tuhst). Wildlife scientists learn about animals and plants. They often study them in the wild.

Wildlife scientists help us learn about **endangered** (en-DAYN-jurd) animals and plants. We also learn how to make sure they do not disappear from the world.

Dr. Ian Stirling

Dr. Ian Stirling has studied polar bears in Hudson Bay, Canada, for over 35 years. He has also learned about **climate** (KLY-muht) **change** in the Arctic.

The Arctic climate is getting warmer. Sea ice is melting. Polar bears stand on sea ice to hunt seals. Dr. Stirling **predicts** that polar bears may disappear from Hudson Bay if there is not enough sea ice.

Hudson Bay

Canada

U.S.A.

Population Prediction

Between 20,000 and 27,000 polar bears live in the wild. Some scientists predict that all polar bears could disappear from Earth within 100 years. The polar bears are dying out because of climate change.

Dr. Stirling began his polar bear **research** in 1970. He wanted to learn about polar bears as part of studying the whole **marine environment** (muh-REEN en-VY-ruhn-muhnt). Dr. Stirling had always dreamed of working in the coldest places on Earth. He was happy to be working with the bears!

LET'S EXPLORE MATH

Hudson Bay Polar Bear Population

Two groups of polar bears live in Hudson Bay: Western Hudson Bay polar bears and Southern Hudson Bay polar bears.

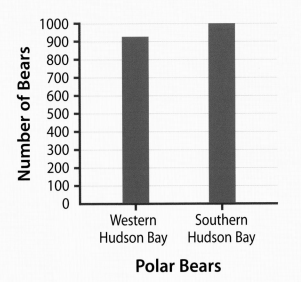

a. About how many more Southern Hudson Bay polar bears are there than Western Hudson Bay polar bears?

Studying Polar Bears

Polar bears can be hard to find. They are often found by spotting their tracks in the snow. Sometimes the bears are on sea ice. They can only be reached by helicopter.

Big Bears

Polar bears are the largest of the bear species.

Length of Polar Bears

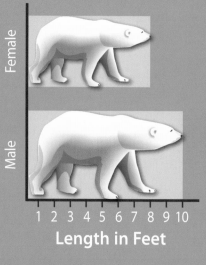

Adult Polar Bears

Female

Male

1 2 3 4 5 6 7 8 9 10

Length in Feet

Polar bears can be dangerous to study. Dr. Stirling puts the bear to sleep first. Then, he measures the bear and tags each ear. He **tattoos** (tah-TOOS) a number on the inside of its lips. He takes out a small tooth from the bear's mouth. He uses the tooth to find out the bear's age. Finally, Dr. Stirling puts a special collar on the bear. The collar means the bear can be tracked.

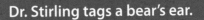

Dr. Stirling tags a bear's ear.

Dr. Stirling counts the number of bears he finds in an area. He wants to know how long they live. He counts how many cubs are born. He catches and tags a group of bears 1 year. Then he catches the same number of bears the next year. He counts the number of untagged bears. Then he can work out how many new bears are being born.

Dr. Stirling is about to collar a female polar bear. Her cub is watching.

In 1 spring season, Dr. Stirling studied 119 **litters** of polar bears.

a. About how many 2-cub litters are there?

b. Which type of litter is there least of?

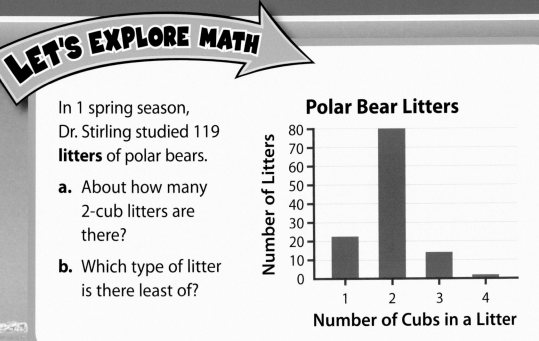

Polar Bear Litters

Number of Litters

80
70
60
50
40
30
20
10
0

1   2   3   4

Number of Cubs in a Litter

Polar bears can be hard to spot in the winter snow. Dr. Stirling gets his **data** between late March and mid-May. This is when the bears are on land ice or are close to the shore. Dr. Stirling may also get his data in summer. Polar bears are easily seen in summer.

Furry Feet

Stiff hairs grow on the soles of a polar bear's feet. These hairs **insulate** (IN-suh-late) the feet and provide **traction** (TRAK-shuhn) on the ice.

How Fast?

Polar bears walk around 3.4 miles per hour (5.5 km/h). When chasing prey, polar bears can run as fast as 25 miles per hour (40 km/h) for short distances.

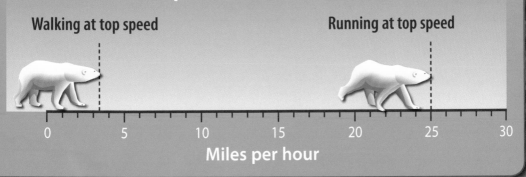

Speed of Polar Bears

Walking at top speed   Running at top speed

0   5   10   15   20   25   30

Miles per hour

The Future of Polar Bears

Dr. Stirling has noticed that Arctic sea ice now melts early at the end of winter. It melts nearly 3 weeks earlier than it did 20 years ago. This means that polar bears have less time to catch food. Female polar bears are having fewer cubs. Cubs that are born are not often **surviving**.

Arctic Winter Ice

In March, 2007, the area of the Arctic ocean covered by ice was 5.7 million square miles (14.7 km^2). Around 20 years ago, the area was 6.1 million square miles (15.7 km^2).

In 2003, Dr. Stirling won an **award** for his work with polar bears. He has written 3 books. He has also written over 200 reports and articles. Dr. Stirling believes that one of the most important parts of being a wildlife scientist is to share his research with people.

More Polar Bear Research

A 2004 *National Geographic* study showed that polar bears weighed about 15% less that year than they did in the 1970s. Can you think why?

Dr. Jane Goodall

Dr. Jane Goodall was born in 1934 in England. When she was a child, Jane's father gave her a toy chimpanzee. She called it Jubilee. When Dr. Goodall grew up, she went to Africa. She studied real chimpanzees.

Chimpanzees are found in 21 African countries.

Africa

Dr. Goodall arrived in Africa in 1957. She met a famous scientist called Dr. Louis Leakey. He asked her to study wild chimpanzees at Gombe National Park in Tanzania. At that time, little was known about chimpanzees. Dr. Goodall had to find out about the ways they did things.

Dr. Louis Leakey

Research from Africa

Dr. Goodall began her research in 1960. The chimpanzees would not let her come close to them at first. She had to study them from a distance. She used **binoculars** to do this. The chimpanzees learned to trust Dr. Goodall after a while. Then she was able to get close to them. At night, Dr. Goodall wrote about all the things that she had seen.

Dr. Goodall learned that chimpanzees are a lot like people. Chimpanzees live in families and in **communities** (kuh-MYU-nuh-teez). They think, and they have feelings. They hug and kiss. Young chimpanzees laugh when they play.

LET'S EXPLORE MATH

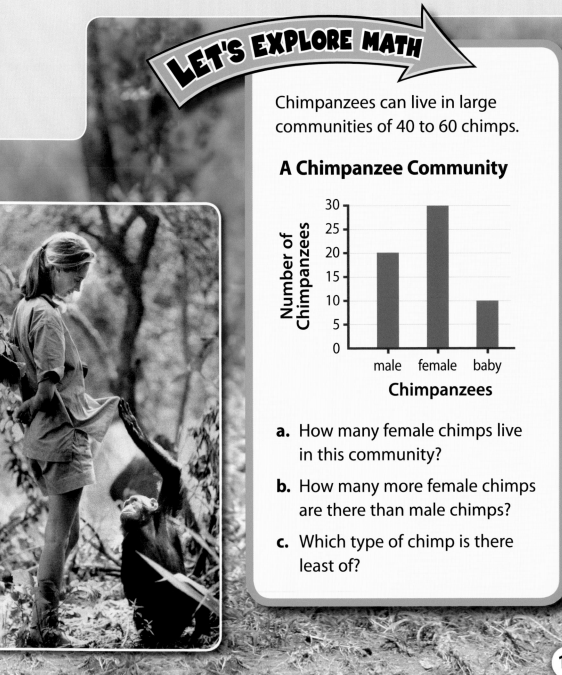

Chimpanzees can live in large communities of 40 to 60 chimps.

A Chimpanzee Community

a. How many female chimps live in this community?

b. How many more female chimps are there than male chimps?

c. Which type of chimp is there least of?

One day, Dr. Goodall made a discovery. It was a very important part of her research. She saw two chimps make tools. They were using tools to catch food. No one thought that chimps could do that.

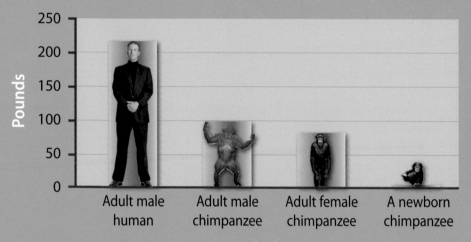

How Much Do They Weigh?

Pounds — Human and Chimpanzees

(Bar graph showing weights: Adult male human ≈ 200; Adult male chimpanzee ≈ 90; Adult female chimpanzee ≈ 75; A newborn chimpanzee ≈ low)

LET'S EXPLORE MATH

Dr. Goodall compared the weights of chimpanzees to an adult male human.

a. Is an adult male human heavier than an adult male chimpanzee?

b. Approximately how many pounds heavier is an adult male chimpanzee than an adult female chimpanzee?

Teaching Others to Help

In 1965, Dr. Goodall started a research center. The center is a place where students help with chimpanzee research. They learn how to study the chimpanzees and record data.

Endangered!

Chimpanzees are an endangered species. At the turn of the twentieth century, at least 1 million wild chimpanzees lived in 25 countries across West and Central Africa. Now, probably between 170,000 and 300,000 wild chimpanzees are left across all of Africa.

Number of Chimpanzees in Africa, 2007

Type of Chimpanzee	Number
Eastern Chimpanzee	76,400–124,600
Central Chimpanzee	70,000–116,000
Western Chimpanzee	21,000–55,000
Nigeria-Cameroon Chimpanzee	5,000–8,000

Dr. Goodall visits the center every year. But she does not do research work there. Instead, she travels the world. She speaks about her work with the chimpanzees.

Making the World Better

Dr. Goodall has also started a program for children and young people. It is called Roots and Shoots. Children and young people learn about wild animals. They also learn about **conservation** (kon-sur-VAY-shuhn) of the environment.

Chimp Conservation

Chimpanzees are hunted for meat. The forests that they live in are being **logged** or farmed. Some chimpanzees are taken from the wild and put in zoos. Dr. Goodall's conservation programs are working toward protecting chimpanzees and their environment.

Dr. Jane Goodall has received over 20 awards for her work. She is also a United Nations Messenger of Peace. She believes that all people can make the world a better place for people and animals.

Dr. Jane Goodall
Time Line

1934 Jane Goodall is born.

1957 She arrives in Africa and meets Dr. Louis Leakey.

1960 She begins her research.

1961 She discovers chimpanzees make tool.

1930   1940   1950   1960   1970

Look at Dr. Jane Goodall's time line.

a. How old was Dr. Jane Goodall when she met Dr. Louis Leakey?

b. How many years after Dr. Goodall arrived in Africa did *National Geographic* magazine publish one of her reports?

c. How old was she when she began the Roots and Shoots program for children?

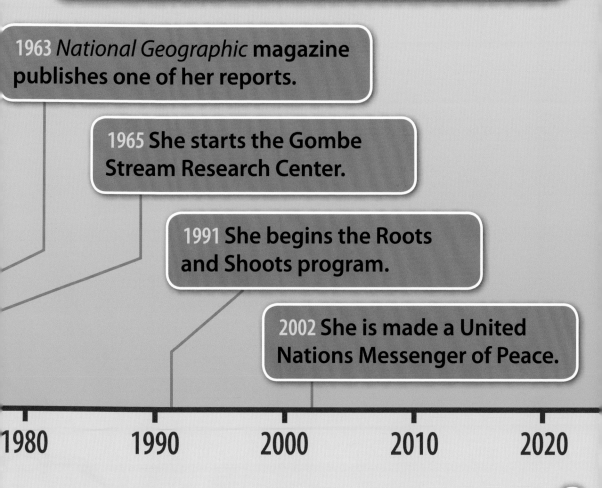

1963 *National Geographic* **magazine publishes one of her reports.**

1965 **She starts the Gombe Stream Research Center.**

1991 **She begins the Roots and Shoots program.**

2002 **She is made a United Nations Messenger of Peace.**

1980   1990   2000   2010   2020

Find That Polar Bear!

Wildlife scientists collected data on the number of polar bears found in the Southern Beaufort Sea area. The table below shows how many bears they studied between 2001 and 2006.

Polar Bears in the Southern Beaufort Sea Area

Year of Study	Number of Polar Bears Studied
2001	137
2002	113
2003	170
2004	285
2005	249
2006	145

Solve It!

a. Use the data in the table and the steps below to create a bar graph.

Step 1: Draw a table that has 6 rows and 6 columns. Make each row and column 1 inch in length and height.

Step 2: Look at the data table. Along the bottom line, label each column with the years of study. Then, underneath the years, write "Years of Study."

Step 3: Look at the data table again. Label the rows on the left by writing 0 at the bottom, 50 on the first row line, and 100 on the second row line. Continue counting by 50 and writing numbers on each row line. Beside the numbers, write "Number of Polar Bears Studied."

Step 4: Look at the data table once more. In 2001, 137 bears were studied. Put a mark in the 2001 column that is an estimate of where 137 would be on the left line. Draw a line across the column. Now color the column. Repeat for the numbers of bears studied in the other years.

Now use the information on the graph to answer these questions.

b. In which year was the largest number of bears studied?

c. In which year was the least number of bears studied?

d. In what year were almost 250 bears studied?

e. What other questions could you ask about the graph?

Glossary

award—a prize or reward for good work

binoculars—a piece of equipment with special glass for each eye that makes distant objects appear closer

climate—the weather conditions of a place or region

climate change—a change in the weather conditions of a place or region that has an effect on the environment

communities—groups of different people or animals living in one place

conservation—the saving of animals or plants from dying out

data—information collected

endangered—in danger of becoming extinct

habitat—the place or area where an animal or plant is found

insulate—to stop heat or cold passing out of something

litters—the babies of animals

logged—cut down by logging companies

marine environment—areas relating to the sea

predicts—says something will happen in the future

research—the collecting of data

surviving—being able to live during or after a difficult time

tattoos—to put a permanent mark on skin

traction—being able to walk on a slippery surface without slipping

wildlife scientist—a person who collects data on animals through study and observation

Index

Let's Explore Math

Page 7:

a. There are about 100 more Southern Hudson Bay polar bears than Western Hudson Bay polar bears.

Page 11:

a. There are 80 2-cub litters.

b. There is the least number of 4 cub litters.

Page 19:

a. 30 female chimps live in this community.

b. There are 10 more female chimps to male chimps.

c. There is the least number of the baby chimps.

Page 21:

a. Yes

b. 18 pounds heavier

Page 27:

a. 23 years old

b. 6 years

c. 57 years old

Problem-Solving Activity

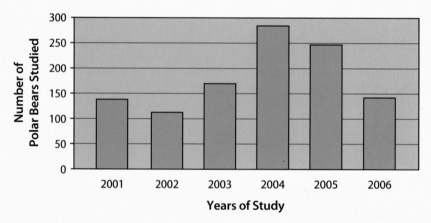

b. The largest number of bears was studied in 2004.

c. The least number of bears was studied in 2002.

d. Almost 250 bears were studied in 2005.

e. Questions will vary.